bug

bug

Yolanda Bonnell

bug
first published 2020 by Scirocco Drama
An imprint of J. Gordon Shillingford Publishing Inc.
© 2020 Yolanda Bonnell

Scirocco Drama Editor: Glenda MacFarlane

Cover art by Chief Lady Bird
Cover design by Doowah Design
Author photo by Graham Isador

Printed and bound in Canada on 100% post-consumer recycled paper.
We acknowledge the financial support of the Manitoba Arts Council and
The Canada Council for the Arts for our publishing program.

Production inquiries to:
yolanda@manidoons.com

Library and Archives Canada Cataloguing in Publication

Title: Bug / Yolanda Bonnell.
Names: Bonnell, Yolanda, 1982- author.
Description: A play.
Identifiers: Canadiana 20200304763 | ISBN 9781927922668 (softcover)
Classification: LCC PS8603.O56 B84 2020 | DDC C812/.6—dc23

J. Gordon Shillingford Publishing
P.O. Box 86, RPO Corydon Avenue, Winnipeg, MB Canada R3M 3S3

*I dedicate this story to all Indigenous women,
2 Spirit and non-binary folks who are struggling
due to the intergenerational effects of colonization.
I see you.*

*To Barbara Kentner. To Tina Fontaine.
To Chantel Moore and Regis Korchinski-Paquette.*

All of our missing and murdered.

*To all of the kwe in my family – especially my niece,
Raina, who I know will change the world.*

Contents

Yolanda Bonnell

Yolanda Bonnell (*She/Her*) is a Queer 2 Spirit Anishinaabe-Ojibwe & South Asian, european mixed performer, playwright and multidisciplinary creator/educator. Originally from Fort William First Nation in Thunder Bay, Ontario (Superior Robinson Treaty territory), Yolanda's arts practice is now based in Tkarón:to. In 2016, Yolanda and Michif (Métis) artist Cole Alvis began manidoons collective, a circle of artists creating Indigenous performance. In February 2020, Yolanda's four-time Dora-nominated solo show *bug* was remounted at Theatre Passe Muraille. She was also a part of Factory Theatre's The Foundry, a creation program for new career writers, where her play, *Scanner,* continues to be developed towards production. In 2018, Yolanda was invited to be part of the Banff Playwrights Lab with her piece *White Girls in Moccasins,* which is now in residency at Buddies in Bad Times Theatre. She was also named one of *NOW Magazine*'s "15 stage artists to watch" with Natasha Greenblatt, with whom she co-wrote *The Election,* which premiered at Theatre Passe Muraille, co-produced by Common Boots Theatre in association with Nightwood Theatre in October 2019. Yolanda proudly bases her practice in land-based creation, drawing on energy and inspiration from the earth and her ancestors.

Acknowledgements / Thank Yous

Chi Miigwetch to

My ancestors and the spirit of that little bug crawling across the sidewalk on Twenty-Second Street.

Laurel Schell, Corrinne Lepage, Elizabeth Staples, Lisa Alves, Angela Blais, Sam Migliazza, Graham Ko

Jessica Lea Fleming, Isaac Thomas, Keith Barker, Brittany Ryan, Olivia Shortt

Mel Hague, Donna-Marie Baratta, Tara Beagan, Victoria Wang, Yvette Nolan, Sarah Garton Stanley, Artie K. Martin

Ashley Bomberry, Aria Evans, Maddie Bautista, Jay Havens, Michel Charbonneau, DJ Classic Roots, Jennifer Kreisberg, Erika Iserhoff

Naomi Campbell, Josephine Ridge, Sammie Gough, Heather Lindsay, Margaret August, Quelemia Sparrow, Nyla Carpenter, Gia Nahmens, Chantal Stormsong Chagnon, Troy Emery Twigg, Tisha Wadsworth, Cara Black Water

Cheryl Silen, Matt Goertz, Shaundra Benincasa, Denise Kurceba-Krawczuk, Gail Bannon, Bess Legarde, Helen Pelletier, Jean Marshall, Leanna Marshall, Mary Magiskan and all of the kwe of Fort William First Nation

Marjorie Chan, Régine Cadet, Andy McKim, Deb Lim

Sanchari Sur, Karyn Recollet, Kelly Boutsalis,
Trisha Dayal, Keira Grant, Christa Couture, Ange Loft,
Kim Senklip Harvey, Lindsay Lachance

Jason Goudreau, Kristina Lemieux, Indrit Kasapi, Aaron
El Sabrout, Milly Bonnell, Mary Bonnell, Sheena Ganth,
Nathenia Bonnell, Raina Bonnell, Jill Carter

All of the youth and women from the unceded
Coast Salish territories, Treaty 7, Kainai First Nation
and Tkarón:to who attended the workshops

Our healers/traditional support workers: Bruce Robinson,
the Tsow-Tun Le Lum Society, Conrad Jones, Audrey Deroy,
Nicole Penak, Michael White, Jenny Blackbird, Mike Ormsby

Our beautiful Elder and Grandmother Pauline Shirt

The Ontario Arts Council, the Toronto Arts Council and
the Canadian Council for the Arts and all of our presenters.

And to Cole Alvis, my artistic partner, director,
dramaturg and so much more. I wouldn't have been able
to get this far and soar this high without you by my side.
Miigwetch/Marsee xo

A Reality

From Reclaiming Power and Place: The Final Report of the National Inquiry into Missing and Murdered Indigenous Women and Girls, Volume 1a

https://www.mmiwg-ffada.ca/final-report/

"In tandem with the residential school system, the child welfare system, therefore, became a site of assimilation and colonization by forcibly removing children from their homes and placing them with non-Indigenous families. Foster and adoptive families were consistently found out of-province, and often out-of-country. Out-of-province or out-of-country adoptions made it extremely challenging for adoptees to be repatriated by their families and communities." (*Page 288*)

"Indigenous women are 4.4 times more likely to have been the legal responsibility of the government (9.1%) than non-Indigenous women (2.1%). This includes being in foster care, group homes, residential school, or youth justice facilities." (*Page 367*)

"For Indigenous girls and 2SLGBTQQIA youth, the dangers associated with moving from one place to another or with being displaced from a safe community are significantly heightened. However, given the extensive violence and abuse experienced by many youth in care, leaving a foster home or other living accommodation may be the only option that seems to exist in order to escape violence." (*Page 560*)

"Further, mental health and addictions issues are often attributed to legacies of colonization and residential schools. Ill health is both a contributing factor to, and result of, higher rates of violence against Indigenous women, girls, and 2SLGBTQQIA people." (*Page 574*)

Playwright's Note

What are we doing to raise up the voices and stories of our sisters?

When women like Barbara Kentner can't walk down a street without being attacked – only to be told that it was a pre-existing condition that took her life rather than the blunt force of a trailer hitch to her abdomen?

When we live in a place where our 15-year-old sister Tina Fontaine, who was failed by the foster care system, is murdered by a white man and an all-white jury finds him not guilty?

When there are thousands of missing and murdered Indigenous women and girls – their cases unsolved – their spirits unrested?

Indigenous women and 2 Spirit folks are often made to feel like we are worthless – that due to the struggle that some of us have with addictions, or mental health issues, our lives don't matter.

The reality of colonial and intergenerational trauma and genocide is consistently ignored because all some people can see is the stereotype that was perpetuated and caused by colonization. Because they don't take enough time to learn the history. Because it's real easy for them to pretend that we've already been erased. Because they think there's a difference between us and the land itself.

So let's tell our stories.

Because the struggle of fighting to be seen or feel like we matter is real. There is a root to our trauma and coping and when we acknowledge that root, then we can encourage it to grow into something more. Something like hope. Hope that we don't have to fight so hard to be seen and heard.

Hope that we will find ways of cultural healing rather than numbing.

Indigenous women, 2 Spirit, trans and non-binary folks are so much more than the stereotype that was created for us. We are made of joy and love. We are defenders. We are Matriarchs and leaders. Lovers and fighters. Flawed and beautiful.

We have to remember that and keep remembering.

Yolanda Bonnell
June 2020

Director's Note

My grandma picked saskatoon berries
My mother makes blankets
I direct this play for the Métis women in my blood

As colonial forces intervene in my matriarchal line
These women prove they are of this place with the power to heal
I make art to celebrate their spirit

Yolanda Bonnell is a truth teller
She makes beautiful what can be devastating
It is ceremony to collaborate with her and our creative team

We all have a role in building meaningful relationships on these
lands and waterways
You are a witness to this performance along with ongoing acts
of colonialism
And we invite you to find yourself inside this play

Marsee

Cole Alvis
June 2020

Foreword

By listening to your story, my story can change.
By listening to your story, I can change.
(Betsy Annahatak, qtd. in TRC 125)

With *bug*, Yolanda Bonnell presents her body as a *vessel* through
which multiple generations of Indigenous women bound by
blood and placenta are offered voice and agency and invited
to speak with, about, and across each other. It is within this
corporeal "lodge" that all times become one as grandmother,
mother, granddaughter, and daughters yet unborn are drawn
together to navigate a complex and specific web of trauma that
has woven itself into the filaments of their DNA (and indeed
into the DNA strands of all Indigenous and racialized peoples
since the advent of the colonial project). Temporally and spatially
unbounded, this web of trauma has altered the shape and course
of ancestral life as it continues to alter the shape and course of
the lives of the descendants who live today and who are yet
to come. Ever mindful of her personal and aesthetic objective
to facilitate healing, Bonnell ushers us with great care through
this psychic web, as she *presences* a daughter's self-loathing,
which has emerged as a logical consequence of parental aban-
donment (*or, more accurately, as a consequence of abduction by the
state*); a mother's self-loathing, which has emerged as a logical
consequence of being judged unfit to care for her child; and the
resultant shadows of anxiety, depression, and fear that darken
the lives of this fragmented family and, indeed, of all Indigenous
peoples who have been removed from their traditional territories
and who (under the Indian Act) continue to exist as legislated
wards of an occupying government.

In somatic metaphor and sonic verse, Yolanda Bonnell

confronts the continuing saga of colonial violence and of white body supremacy,[1] curating an "irreconcilable space" (see Garneau 26–27)[2] of healing for the Indigenous witness of her work through her own witness of and corporeal reckoning with a shared legacy. At the same time, Bonnell skillfully withholds access from settler witnesses to this Indigenous space of healing. For this audience, she constructs a liminal threshold that is at once spatially inscribed and immaterial. Within the space to which they have been restricted, Euro-Canadian audiences are confronted with their own legacy of "intergenerational perpetration" (Robinson 63)[3] – a legacy Canadians have yet to address in any lasting and meaningful way.

The residential schools to which generations of Indigenous children were spirited away and within which so many were

1   African American trauma-therapist Resmaa Menakem suggests that we replace the term "White Supremacy" with the term *White Body Supremacy.* "White Supremacy," he posits, carries no somatic resonance: "We tried to make our brains think better about race [but] the real battle is inside our bodies." If we continue to theorize racism (casting it as an intellectual conundrum), it becomes too easy for the White body of the present moment to reflexively shrug off accountability. The White body may be "thinking better about race," hence, that body can say to itself "[this is] not me." Menakem argues that genocide, land theft, enslavement and colonialism live in the White Body, passed down through the generations of Europeans, who fleeing from their own traumas (war, bloodshed, oppression, environmental degradation, starvation, disease, etc.), carried these unaddressed traumas with them and visited these upon the "Bodies of Culture" (non-White, eminently **human** bodies) whom they encountered, as they laboured to claim and build a "new world" on stolen lands through the labour of stolen bodies. Menakem further argues that White people need to curate spaces and active processes through which to address their own inheritance and to deal with "the embodiment of race" – an ingrained (and perhaps, now subconscious) ontological certainty that "to be White is to be human" and, consequently, to be not White is to be something other-than-human (Menakem np).
2   Metis scholar-curator David Garneau conceives of "irreconcilable spaces of Aboriginality." He imagines them as "intellectual spaces that exist apart from a non-Indigenous gaze and interlocution. The idea is to signal to non-Indigenous spectators the fact that intellectual activity is occurring without their knowledge; that is, "without their knowledge," as in without their being aware, and "without their knowledge" in the sense of intellectual activities based on Native rather than Western epistemologies" (26–27).
3   I borrow this term from Sto:Lo scholar Dylan Robinson (63) who calls upon settler Canadians to cease their inactivity not only by learning about and passively acknowledging responsibility for an ongoing history of bad faith, treaty violation, and genocidal acts but also by mobilizing a score of ongoing and concrete actions through which to operationalize redress and so end their collective assault upon the minds and bodies of Indigenous humans and upon the biotas that they steward and that sustain us all.

miseducated, exploited, and abused may now, after 150 years, have ceased to operate. But despite these closures, Indigenous children continue to be taken from their homes by the Canadian state and placed into foster homes where, more often than not, the physical and emotional abuse once visited upon their parents and grandparents in residential schools is replicated in these twenty-first-century systems of "care." Degradation, physical violence, and sexual exploitation continue to pervade the experience of these stolen children, as their parents – now bereft and condemned as "unworthy" – struggle to heal from their own scars and struggle to rekindle the necessary fires within to maintain hope and to fight for their safe return.

Degradation, physical violence, and sexual exploitation have pervaded and disfigured the colonial psyche also. In 2019, Canada's prime minister *mocked* a young Indigenous woman who had raised and paid $1500 to attend a fundraising dinner at which he was speaking. "Mr. Trudeau, people at Grassy Narrows are suffering from mercury poisoning," she told him. "You committed [yourself and your nation] to addressing this crisis" (Global News, "Trudeau" np). Amidst laughter and applause from his supporters, Canada's leading man addressed her concerns with these words, "Thank you for your donation." Only months later, when the Final Report of the National Inquiry into Missing and Murdered Indigenous Women and Girls (MMIWG) was released, Prime Minister Justin Trudeau promised that Canada would break its historic inertia and begin to act to protect the rights and wellbeing of Indigenous girls and women and of 2SLGBTQQIA people without acknowledging the centuries-old campaign of attack on Indigenous women as "genocide." At a subsequent gathering of women, he observed that the authors of the report had "*found* that the tragic violence that Indigenous women and girls have experienced *amounts to genocide*" (Global News with Connolly np, emphasis mine). Questions around how *he* (as this nation's leader and representative) might characterize the violence *his* nation has visited upon Indigenous bodies, minds, and spirits for the past 150 years remain unanswered. Are we to see these things as "business as usual" – a logical consequence of "breathing while Indigenous"? Tomato, tomahto… Indigenous, non-Indigenous… Perhaps we *are* hearing the same story, but our reception of that story in this historical moment cannot be reconciled.

It is understandable, perhaps, that settler Canadians approach Bonnell's work with their own agenda. Certainly, they expect to be educated, to be *edified*; possibly, some hope to experience a momentary relief as the weight of intergenerational perpetration is released in a teary trickle or a fleeting moment of sympathy for the "plight" of the characters who presence themselves in Bonnell's body. Perhaps, too, a feeling of settler-vindication might be anticipated, as Bonnell's future Elder basks in the glow of her ancestors, inspirited by their love, and lifted by hope. "All's well that ends well," they might declare. "Nothing more is needed from us."

But this is not how *bug* has been engineered to function. In this historical moment, Yolanda Bonnell and the manidoons collective have created a container in which to push against the institutional constraints and the institutionalized expectations of Canadian audiences around "theatre." They have created a dual ceremony[4] through the curation of "irreconcilable space" in which the epigenetic transgenerational legacies of embodied trauma (Indigenous) and sustained perpetration (non-Indigenous) are presenced and severally addressed.

In performance, Bonnell flips the colonial space of seeing (the *theatron*), inviting heretofore marginalized bodies to occupy

---

4   Indeed, ceremony sits in the very bones of this play. In the process of its creation, *bug* reconfigures the institution of commercial theatre in Canada and pushes back against its infrastructure. Bonnell and the manidoons collective privilege the health and safety of their artists, curating the spaces of devising and rehearsal as spaces of ceremony in which action is governed by the Seven Grandfather Teachings of the Anishinaabeg (Respect, Love, Humility, Honesty, Bravery, Truth, and Wisdom). Hence, rehearsal periods are longer, while rehearsal days are shorter; artists are encouraged to bring their lives and entire human experience into the space of co-creation, as they begin the workday with a talking circle; the spaces in which the piece is performed are appropriately acknowledged and their caretakers honoured; and audiences are invited after every performance to sit with the artists to debrief and converse (Sur np). In 2020, Bonnell excited controversy by enacting a courageous refusal and requesting that White critics refrain from reviewing the show. Traditionally, mainstream critics – by and large, White and by and large, male (see Nolan np) – have held and continue to wield no small degree of power over the life (and perhaps, reception) of a production. Here, too, Bonnell flips the script, restoring to the communities for whom she creates this work respect and authority in their role as final arbiter of the work's merit: as a performative mechanism of healing for and by Indigenous people, *bug* requires and invites community consultation and feedback, rather than a colonial stamp of approval or disapprobation.

an inner circle from which to fulfill the role of witness and so travel with her and the women she carries through those dark spaces where trauma is born into the luminescence of hope. Non-Indigenous witnesses are invited to seat themselves in the margins *outside* the ceremonial circle. Here, they are invited to encounter *bug* in a different way, as Bonnell neatly flips the script, challenging them to reckon with their own legacy and to activate their own healing. Indigenous peoples have our own work to do, as Bonnell shows us. And we're doing it. Settler-Canadians have their work to do – their own poisons to purge.

First, indicting settler-Canadian witnesses for their collusion in a racist system, which justifies violence against "other" humans by refusing to recognize those "others" as human ("And no one cares / Because they are nothing but insects…"), Bonnell flips her performative mirror, reconfiguring the reflected image: now, the non-Indigenous "actor" has been recast as an infestation that poisons the Indigenous body and feasts upon a carcass, rendered virulent by colonial depredation. In her mapping of the dual manifestations of colonial disease (and the resultant Indigenous *dis-ease*), Bonnell offers to the colonial host a possibility of healing. Outside and apart from the inner circle, colonial witnesses are not only confronted with the slippage of their own humanity but also invited to investigate the pathways they will need to follow and the actions they will need to perform to recover wholeness and reclaim that discarded humanity.

bug's "bug" is the conductor of this dual ceremony, *presenced* in Bonnell's body as both "other" and self as she cycles through multiple manifestations. With each manifestation, she offers new possibilities, as she reminds us to remember the dualities that govern our existence and the possibilities these dualities afford – possibilities of re-righting and re-writing the world we have made and by which we are made. Appearing as the firefly, she lights this world with wonder and gladdens the heart of a little girl. As "Glowie," she carries the child's secrets, teaching her to dance and reminding all of us that even in the darkest places, signs and wonders still abide, inviting us into their light. "Glowie" is safety and satiation – easing a relentless hunger for home and safety.

Alternatively, bug presents herself as a manifestation of craving – an "infection" that insinuates itself under the skin as she clouds our senses and teaches us to reach for immoderate quantities of poison (alcohol, drugs, unhealthy relationships, etc.) to sate our longings for the warmth, love, and safety of home. So nourished, she grows by imperceptible degrees into an addiction that – once thwarted in its cravings – expresses itself as a maddening itch that threatens to devour its host body – the unwitting and unwilling host. Like the spider who painstakingly spins her web, this bug is patient and painstaking. She is dogged resilience, but she is an eater of hope and a bringer of death.

And "bug" is the inspiritor[5] of this performative ceremony. Of this inspiritor, Yolanda Bonnell says, "I almost stepped on it. And that was that moment when I was like, 'does it know?' Is it aware of its space in the world? How does it view itself in comparison to these giant creatures that are walking around it? *And then the correlation between that and the treatment of Indigenous women was not lost on me"* (Theatre Passe Muraille np, emphasis added). This bug is the manifestation of the dehumanization of every Indigenous woman by those desperate strangers who stumbled with all their desperate cravings, fears, and fantasies onto her territories and settled themselves there. She is every Indigenous grandmother, aunty, mother, and daughter, and she struggles on despite a centuries-old campaign to eradicate her and so eradicate the future of her nations. She too is dogged resilience. She is the resilience that has woven itself alongside hunger, dislocation, loss, wounding, and re-membered trauma into a bundle, which constitutes the embodied legacy of Indigenous peoples (past, present, and yet to be born). She carries the hope of our nations in her hands, in her breasts, in her songs, in her smiles, in her tears, in her voice, and in her gestures. Despite all, she continues to nurture new life in her womb and to fight for each new life she has delivered into the world.

In a recent podcast, African American trauma-therapist

---

5   Miss Uta Hagen, herself a twentieth-century "inspiritor" of multiple genera-tions of performers in North America, identified her husband Harold Berghof as her inspiritor on the dedication page of her 1991 book *A Challenge for the Actor*. For me the term connotes a medium which not only inspires the creative agent but also overtakes, magnifies, and uplifts the spirit of that agent. In this con-text, then, the bug that inspired Bonnell's initial somatic investigations into the psycho-spiritual lives of multiple generations of Indigenous women from one family realizes herself here as the "bug" who, through all her manifestations, presences herself as conduit within and conductor of a ceremonial event.

Resmaa Menakem reminded his auditors that while trauma is the inheritance held within racialized bodies, teaching us of our unworthiness, this inheritance is not (and does not have to be) our "destiny" (np). And Yolanda Bonnell's play (on page or stage) activates this powerful truth. With *bug,* she carries us through a process of reconciliation[6] – a protected process that lives inside an "irreconcilable space of Aboriginality" – a space which she has operationalized within the space of a colonial institution. *bug* charts a difficult path upon which the traumatized body retraces its steps and revisits each site of wounding to lay down an offering of healing, forgiveness, and release. It activates an embodied return to right relationship with self, family, community, and nation. It carries us home.

And with Bonnell, we are "Glowing."

Jill Carter
Tkaron:to, June 2020

Jill Carter (Anishinaabe/Ashkenazi) is a theatre practitioner and researcher, currently cross appointed to the Centre for Drama, Theatre and Performance Studies; the Transitional Year Programme; and Indigenous Studies at the University of Toronto.

---

6   I do not use the word "reconciliation" to denote the popular, political notion of reconciliation between Canadians and Indigenous peoples. The reconciliation I speak of here is the relational work Indigenous peoples are already beginning to do by and for and amongst themselves: this is the work of relational repair within the self, between family members, community members, and Indigenous nations. This is the work of relational repair between Indigenous peoples and the biotas that have sustained and been stewarded by Indigenous peoples across these territories for thousands of years.

Works Cited

Garneau, David. "Imaginary Spaces of Conciliation and Reconciliation: Art, Curation, and Healing." *Arts of Engagement: Taking Aesthetic Action in and beyond the Truth and Reconciliation Commission of Canada.* Eds. Keavy Martin, Dylan Robinson, David Garneau, et. al. Waterloo: Wilfrid Laurier University Press, 2016. 21-41.

Global News. "Trudeau Apologizes after Telling First Nations Mercury Poisoning Protester, 'Thank you for your donation.'" 27 March 2019. Updated 28 March 2019. https://globalnews.ca/news/5104937/justin-trudeau-protester-liberal-fundraiser/ Last Accessed 17 March 2020.

Global News with Amanda Connolly. "Trudeau Changes Course, Says 'Genocide' When Citing MMIWG Report's Findings." 3 June 2019. https://globalnews.ca/news/5349137/justin-trudeau-genocide-mmiwg-report/ Last Accessed 17 March 2020.

Hagen, Uta. *A Challenge for the Actor.* New York: Scribner, 1991.

Menakem, Resmaa. "Notice the Rage; Notice the Silence." *On Being with Krista Tippet.* 04 June 2020. https://onbeing.org/programs/resmaa-menakem-notice-the-rage-notice-the-silence/ Last Accessed 19 June 2020.

Nolan, Yvette. "Why It Matters Who Reviews Indigenous Theatre." *CBC Arts.* 19 February 2020. https://www.cbc.ca/arts/why-it-matters-who-reviews-indigenous-theatre-1.5467785/ Last Accessed 18 June 2020.

Robinson, Dylan. "Intergenerational Sense, Intergenerational Responsibility." *Arts of Engagement: Taking Aesthetic Action in and beyond the Truth and Reconciliation Commission of Canada.* Eds. Keavy Martin, Dylan Robinson, David Garneau, et. al. Waterloo: Wilfrid Laurier University Press, 2016. 43-65.

Sur, Sanchari. "Decolonizing Theatre Practice as a Playwright and Performer: A Conversation with Yolanda Bonnell." *Intermission: Where All Great Theatre Discussions Happen.* 24 February 2020. https://www.intermissionmagazine.ca/features/decolonizing-theatre-practice-as-a-playwright-and-performer-a-conversation-with-yolanda-bonnell/ Last Accessed18 June 2020.

Theatre Passe Muraille. "Yolanda Bonnell in Conversation with Ange Loft about the Creation of *bug*." Posted 8 February 2020. https://www.passemuraille.ca/bug-blog/ Last Accessed 4 March 2020.

The Truth and Reconciliation Commission of Canada (TRC). *What We Have Learned: Principles of Truth and Reconciliation.* The Final Report of the Truth and Reconciliation Commission of Canada. Ottawa: TRC, 2015. http://nctr.ca/assets/reports/Final%20Reports/Principles_English_Web.pdf Last Accessed 19 June 2020.

Production History

bug began development at Humber School for the Creative and Performing Arts and has since been developed with Native Earth Performing Arts (Weesageechak Festival), Buddies in Bad Times Theatre (Mel Hague, Rhubarb Festival Director & Company Dramaturg), Summerworks Festival, Native Women in the Arts, The Collaborations at National Arts Centre, and Luminato Festival with support from Toronto Arts Council, Ontario Arts Council and Canada Council for the Arts.

The development process continued with presentation on Coast Salish Territories during Intrepid Theatre's UNO Fest (May 2018) in Victoria, BC and rEvolver Festival (May 2018) in Vancouver, BC in preparation for the world premiere on Dish with One Spoon Territory (Tkarón:to) at the Luminato Festival (June 2018).

bug has since been presented on Treaty 7 Territory at High Performance Rodeo and Kainai First Nation High School (January 2019) and Superior Robinson Treaty Territory at Cambrian Players with storytelling workshops in Fort William First Nation (September/October 2019).

In 2019, *bug* was nominated for four Dora Mavor Moore Awards for the manidoons collective / Luminato presentation:

Outstanding New Play

Outstanding Performance in a Lead Role

Outstanding Lighting Design

Outstanding Theatre Production

A remount was performed at Theatre Passe Muraille in Tkarón:to, co-presented with manidoons collective and Native Earth Performing Arts in February 2020.

Production team

bug created and performed by Yolanda Bonnell

director and producer: Cole Alvis

stage manager: Gia Nahmens

voiceover by: Sadie Buck

movement coach: Aria Evans

dramaturg: Yvette Nolan

scenography: Jay Havens

lighting designer: Michel Charbonneau

sound design: Maddie Bautista

production manager: Deb Lim

music composed by: DJ Classic Roots & Jennifer Kreisberg

stitchers: Kinoo Arcentales & Chelsea Reinders

set construction: Tim Hill

associate producers: Lisa Alves & Olivia Shortt

producing consultant: Kristina Lemieux

outside eye / facilitator: Ashley Bomberry

knowledge keeper: Pauline Shirt

bug was created on the land of Tkarón:to, the traditional territory of the Anishinaabeg, the Mississaugas of Credit River, the Haudenosaunee; Six Nations Confederacy and the Wendat.

manidoons collective

manidoons

manidoons collective is a circle of artists creating Indigenous performance. The artistic leadership includes Yolanda Bonnell (Anishinaabe-Ojibwe & South Asian, european mixed) and Cole Alvis (Métis-Chippewa, Irish & English) both based in Tkarón:to. The collective is currently touring *bug* across Turtle Island (North America) while developing new works by Yolanda Bonnell, including *White Girls in Moccasins, Scanner,* and *My Sister's Rage.* manidoons collective recognizes the importance of collaborating with Indigenous communities, specifically Indigenous women, 2-Spirit, trans, and non-binary storytellers.

bug

**A solo piece of storytelling through movement
and a loud Native woman's voice**

*Be fearless
Be bold
Be open
You are channelling;
Be safe
Be hopeful*

THE GIRL
an Indigenous woman of any age

MANIDOONS
*a creature, contorted,
distorted and unsettling*

THE MOTHER
*The Girl's Mother – any Indigenous Mother,
yours, mine*

ANCESTORS/ELDER
*they are embedded into every word of this
story and will manifest in voice and body*

Production Notes

BUG is a piece of physical storytelling as much as it is text-based. I encourage the use of body / gesture / dance / movement for any or all aspects of the story. The indications of physical scores are strongly suggested to heighten that specific text and / or area of the story.

TIME is deconstructed and leaps through memories. We are here and there and yesterday and tomorrow. Past. Present. Future. Sometimes THE GIRL recounts her memories and sometimes she lives in and becomes the memories. This is to say that her present and her Mother's present can simultaneously exist. She is, first and foremost, the storyteller.

MANIDOONS was born of colonialism and is made up of the energies of intergenerational trauma and addictions.

DRUG USE. I never mention which specific drug THE GIRL is addicted to. Every substance addiction has their own ways of affecting or poisoning their person. I did draw heavy inspiration from oxycodone use as it was quite heavy in my community but I also wanted to keep it open so it remained accessible. I leave the choice to you.

HEALERS. I encourage the hiring of healers or traditional support workers with medicines at any performance. As this story deals with some hard truths, it is our responsibility as storytellers in this artistic ceremony to ensure the safety of our witnesses – especially our Indigenous sisters, 2 Spirit and non-binary family.

PROTOCOL. We welcome. We sing. We presence. We give autonomy. We create a space where our witnesses feel comfortable and safe.

The following creation story/land acknowledgement was gifted to us by our Elder, Pauline Shirt, and then written by Yolanda Bonnell. It is meant to be performed as a pre-show by Indigenous youth or recited at the end of the protocol speeches.

Thousands of years ago

Prior to human activity here on what we call Turtle Island

There was a gathering.

This gathering was made up of the smallest insects and the largest animals who put aside their many differences to discuss what was being foretold in the winds.

From the bee and the spider to buffalo and bears, these creatures travelled from all across the land and gathered together at a Great Lake.

It was there they discussed the coming of the Anishinaabe people.

Humans who would be protectors of the lands and waters and all living beings in the cycle of life.

The creatures agreed that they would make way for our people – that they would ensure these Indigenous people would have food and lodging and be taken care of.

That we are all taking care of each other.

And so, the humans arrived and lived with the land.

Different tribes and nations began to inhabit Turtle Island.

To the West and North, there were the Coast Salish people and the Cree.

To the far North, the Inuit.

To the East, the Mi'kmaq.

To the South, the Maya and the Seminole.

And here, *the Anishinaabeg, the Mississaugas, the Haudenosaunee – Six Nations Confederacy and the Wendat.

As well as many, many other nations – some we may not even know about.

Our people recognized that we are all a part of the life cycle.

We are no different than the grass we walk on, the water we drink or the animals we hunt.

This cycle is what feeds and takes care of us and enables us to feed and take care of others.

These nations will change depending on the territory the performance is happening on.

CIRCLES

Drumbeat.

Ancestors move through time and presence themselves.

Conjuring our story.

The ancestors dance – a tree grows and dies and grows and dies and continues to cycle.

An Elder speaks:

What you don't understand is
Where it came from
You don't understand why
The root
That grew into a tree of poison and self-loathing
What you don't understand is
How difficult it is to navigate the branches
When everyone wants to cut down the tree
The tree is sick
What you don't understand
Is that the tree is sick
The poison cycled so much
It became embedded

Into our bark

Sickness was planted in us

And we

We are trying to get well

Everything is heavier

Harder

What you don't understand

Is that trauma

Set us up to fail

Like the policies

That failed

What you don't understand is

How resilient we are

What you don't understand is

How important it is that we live

Keep living

Despite the poison of trauma that runs in our veins

The tree may be sick

But our ancestors are lush green leaves

That continue to give us life

> *THE GIRL is born in this cycle and speaks from within it.*
>
> *She is here because of the strength of her ancestors.*
>
> *Breath.*

Yolanda Bonnell as The Girl, evoking the story as the Elder speaks;
"our ancestors are lush green leaves / That continue to give us life."
Photograph by Dahlia Katz.

REMEMBER

THE GIRL: Hi

Beat.

Um ... I'm scared

I'm scared that she's going to forget me

That she's going to forget my eyes

My hands

My touch on her skin

I'm afraid that she won't hear my voice, you know?

I just ...

I don't want her to end up like m –

Become MANIDOONS.

MANIDOONS ONE: BLUE PAVEMENT

MANIDOONS: Shhh – can you hear it?

Crawling

Crawling on the

Blue pavement

Crawling

On the

Floors

Manidoons at the rock; "Shhh – can you hear it?" Photograph by Dahlia Katz.

On her skin

Making her

Making her move

The sounds of escape

The pitter

Pitter

Of helplessness

The patter

Patter of despair

The tip and the toe of running towards the thing
she loves the most in this world

Of thirst and

Need and

Want and –

FIREFLIES

Become human.

*THE GIRL is young and on a path in a forest
on her reservation.*

*She giggles and catches something in her
hands.*

THE GIRL: I used to call them glowies.

And they were the only bugs I couldn't talk to.

Because they always flew so far away from me.

Dancing with fireflies; "I used to call them glowies." Photograph by
Gilad Cohen.

She dances with the fireflies.

All I wanted to do was catch one and tell it my secrets.

She whispers a secret into her hands.

They were so small though – so tiny. It seemed impossible.

There *was* a part of me that wanted to squish it, you know? Squish it and take its light and rub it all over me so that I would glow in the dark too.

But when I saw them in the sky, blinking with their light – I just wanted to see where they were gonna light up next

So, I followed their trail; guessed their path.

Nothing else mattered but seeing it light up again.

Beat.

Did you know that some types of female fireflies can't fly?

I mean, what's the point of being a firefly if you can't fly?

I caught one once

I was so sure

THE GIRL slowly and sneakily opens her hand and then eats what is there – or what is not there – it travels through her body and she feels herself being yanked backwards.

MY GIRL

A support group.

THE MOTHER sits in a chair.

THE MOTHER:

Puts one finger out, then another and another and another until four are up.

This is my fourth time.

Number four.

Fourth time's the charm!

Is that – isn't that what they say?

This is it.

This is IT.

No more after this.

I'm telling you, boy.

I'm done.

I'm tired.

I'm old.

Ahh, you want me to talk, eh?

You always want me to talk.

Whatchu want me to talk about this time?

Beat.

My girl?

My girl.

My girl was perfect.

The Mother sharing her stories in group; "Fourth time's the charm! Is that – isn't that what they say?" Photograph by Gilad Cohen.

She was – she was perfect.

You know, she barely even cried when she was a baby.

Swear to God – that baby barely even cried.

She'd make these little – like these squeak noises.

Like a little mouse.

My little mouse baby.

She was so small too

Just –

She indicates baby's size.

You know?

I remember havin' her at the hospital up there and – and even the nurses, you know?

Even the nurses would say "Oh she's so tiny. Look how tiny she is. So small."

Waving their white fingers in her face.

I was scared at first cuz you know, I thought there mighta been somethin' – somethin' wrong with her.

Cuz you know – we didn't know … back then.

We didn't know what we were doin'.

But they let me take her home.

And she had her own crib and everything.

Beat – she looks to someone in the circle.

Hey, can I have a smoke?

They didn't say we couldn't smoke here, right?

Can I have one?

> *She takes two cigarettes, puts one behind her ear and walks away.*

Thanks.

SMILE

> *A memory.*
>
> *THE GIRL moves through the image and the fog of memory while she describes it.*

THE GIRL: There's this picture that I have.

I don't know where it came from.

I think I've just always had it.

It's of my Mother

Me

And my Auntie

And we're outside

It's summer

The sun is bright

And my Mother is squinting but her face is so beautiful

She's smiling

She has a big smile

So big

It almost takes up the entire frame

And she's holding me with one arm and blocking the sun with the other

And her head is tilted to one side

She looks young

She *was* young

I was young

I was maybe a year – maybe two years

I look small and dark and wiggly – like I wouldn't stop moving

But I was smiling

The both of us were smiling

And my Auntie is standing beside her leaning over at me

Trying to get me to grab her finger or something.

And her hair is so long and dark and it covers almost all of her body.

Her mouth is active.

She is laughing or something

We all look so much alike.

    Beat.

    Repetitive gesture.

Every time I look at that picture, all I can see is my Mother's smile.

Every time I look at that picture, my Mother's smile covers my whole body.

Every time I look at that picture, I wonder what was making her smile.

Was it me?

Was it the sun?

Or was it something else?

A living room.

I was watching her

On the day she let them take me

> *THE GIRL sits and watches her Mother on the couch as a five-year-old.*

I watched her

She was passed out on the couch

A spider fell from the roof and landed on her head

She didn't even notice

It creeped slowly across her forehead

Around her eyebrows

Down her cheek

I sat and watched

I wanted to see her eat it

You know that thing – where they say you eat like a whole bunch of spiders in your lifetime while you sleep??

That's what I wanted.

I wanted to see her eat that spider.

Or

The spider eat her.

She sits and watches for a moment.

Neither happened though. It disappeared behind her body.

But I like to think that spider is still attached to her somewhere.

She is being taken away.

Buried

In her skin.

DISPLACEMENT

THE GIRL begins her journey through various foster homes as a physical score or repetitive gesture.

THE GIRL: Then

I was taken

Scooped

Snatched

Picked up and moved

Like a game piece

Sometimes I got to stay with my Auntie when she could take me but she couldn't always take me.

Taken

Scooped and snatched

Picked up and moved somewhere else

No one ever noticed me

They didn't see

They didn't care

Sneakily.

I could do whatever I wanted...

> *She reaches for the beer on a high counter.*
>
> *She physicalizes through gesture each potential new addiction.*

I had my first taste of beer when I was 8.

It was disgusting.

I was drinking wine and vodka by the time I was 12.

They didn't care

I had my first cigarette when I was 11.

I picked it out of the ashtray on the coffee table and had to light it on the stove.

I didn't even cough.

I was chain smoking less than a year later.

They didn't see

I smoked my first joint when I was 14.

My foster sister handed it to me.

She said I didn't have to.

I wanted to

So I did

I fell in love with the feeling

They didn't ...

Breath.

I tried my first ... (*Gasp.*)

She is yanked back.

When I was ... (*Gasp.*)

She is yanked back.

It made me feel ...

I felt ...

I feel ...

She is suddenly somewhere else.

Confusion.

I feel like I'm supposed to be doing some –

Become MANIDOONS.

MANIDOONS TWO: BLUE SKY

MANIDOONS: Shhh

Do you hear that?

It's so loud

Loud and pounding

Those raindrops

Thundering sobs from the

dark blue sky

I made it across the

Across the room

Before it began

But not before I tasted her

Infected her

She doesn't know I'm here, yet

It just takes so long to

Long to

Crawl

To slither

I wish

I wish I had wings instead

ANTS

Become human.

A bedroom.

THE GIRL: I used to hoard food under my bed so that Pat and Larry, my foster parents, wouldn't catch on. So like … OK

THE GIRL sits on her bed.

In one night, I would make myself a sandwich – no but like a *stacked* sandwich. Then I would grab a plastic grocery bag and fill it with all sorts of shit. It was just a big bag of food and I stuffed whatever I didn't eat under the bed. I had half-full bags and bags with crumbs and loose bits of things I didn't eat. It was a food bag graveyard under there and I just never did anything about it. They just kept piling up.

Of course a smell crept in from God knows whatever food was under there but Pat never came in to check on me so no one really noticed.

THE GIRL slowly spreads herself out as the ants carry her away.

And then, one night I was lying in bed and I realized I was watching an ant on the wall, then two, and a third one. I imagined a horde of them trying to carry my big body back to the hill. To consume me. I sort of ... wished for it.

How many would that take!?

Thunder – she wakes up from a nightmare and almost falls out of bed.

AUNTIE

Comfort.

My Auntie

The Girl being carried away by ants; "I imagined a horde of them trying to carry my big body back to the hill." Photograph by Kaytee Dalton.

She used to sing me to sleep at night when I stayed with her ... because nightmares.

A lullaby.

I would wake up, screaming.

She would tell me to pray to make them go away, that the nightmares weren't real. Then she would tell me not to worry. That our ancestors were watching over me so that nothing could *really* hurt me.

So I would say the Our Father, I would say the Hail Mary, and she would tuck me in and sing:

> *She sings "Twinkle Twinkle" in Anishinaabemowin.**

Anangoohns anangoohns waasikose

indoowaanendam awenen giin...

It's pretty much the only Ojibwe I know.

No one else taught me any of it.

> *MANIDOONS begins creeping up through one of her hands.*

My Mother, she –

> *She is again, yanked backwards.*

My Mother, she –

---

* Anishinaabemowin is spoken in a wide variety of geographical locations and therefore has many different dialects. This is what I remember as a child. I encourage you to use your own language or dialect if at all possible.

HUMILIATION

> *A support group.*
>
> *THE MOTHER sits in a chair.*

THE MOTHER: I watched her.

> I useta watch her play in the yard.
>
> Her dark hair just curly, you know?
>
> Those curls, they –
>
> Well – she don't have them no more.
>
> I guess she musta –
>
> Musta grown outta them
>
> They grow up fast, eh?
>
> So fast.

> *Beat.*

> (*To one of the witnesses.*) Hey, you got kids?

> (*YES:*) They grow up fast, eh?
>
> (*NO:*) Well let me tell ya, boy. They grow up fast.

> And it's tough, you know?
>
> Tryina raise em
>
> Tryina raise em right.
>
> Tryina … build em to fight.
>
> To fight back.
>
> Fight everyone in this – this racist city we live in.
>
> You know someone spit on me once.

Yeah.

Spit right on me while I was sittin' on the corner.

Just tryina get some coffee money.

Beat.

"Drunk bogan slut!"

She spits.

And his friends just laughed.

There's something so humiliating about being bullied by teenagers when you're an adult.

I just wanted to get up and fight him. I wanted to fight all of them. Just fuckin knock them the fuck out.

But I didn't.

I just sat there – in my humiliation … with spit on my sweater.

Didn't even wipe it off!

KWE

A memory.

THE GIRL: I was 12 years old when I felt a penis for the first time!

My boyfriend took my hand and placed it on his crotch and held it there while it got hard

And it felt like a stick or something and then I got scared that it was gonna break off in my hand

And I did not wanna be that girl in school who broke off her boyfriend's penis

On the bus.

He was a few years older than me

But I always looked older than I was

And when we did it, he was like "Uuugghh … I've never been with an Indian before."

And it didn't hurt

You know, it felt good … to be wanted

That's a feeling I remember

The feeling of being … desired

By anyone

I

Began

To crave it…

Movement score to all the boys.

Dennis lived down the street from me – he liked to choke me when we did it

Randy went to the rival public school – he kissed too much. I always left with my cheeks wet

David was a friend of my cousin who came to visit the summer – he didn't like to look at my face

Mitchell was a carnie who only liked to look at my face

Aaron always gave me hickies so people knew that I. Was. His

Scott only wanted blowjobs

Ian liked to hit

Brad always bit

and John!!

> *Violence.*
>
> *She is forced to bend over.*
>
> *Breath.*

But I let them

I let them all use me

Use me up

Hurt me

Love me

> *She is being pulled slowly across the floor by her braid.*

There's something – something about the struggle.

Of tiny bugs.

Helpless.

Slowly creeping across sidewalks.

Are they aware that they can be crushed at any moment?

That, at any second – someone – some person could potentially just – step on them?

Squish them into oblivion and walk away – with
a bit of their remains on the bottom of a shoe?

She sits up, holding her braid up in the air.

And they are totally powerless to stop it.

The inevitability of such a small creature in such
a giant place.

They never stood a chance.

She is –

Swatted.

Slapped.

Squished.

Flicked.

Poisoned.

Choked.

Begins slowly and then builds in intensity.

Swatted.

Slapped.

Squished.

Flicked.

Poisoned.

Choked.

Swatted.

Slapped.

The Girl being held up by her braid; "they never stood a chance."
Photograph by Dahlia Katz.

Squished.

Flicked.

Poisoned.

Choked.

Swatted.

Slapped.

Squished.

Flicked.

Poisoned.

Choked.

Stepped on!

> *She is flattened – stepped on.*

> *Breath.*
> *She gathers herself.*

And no one cares.

Because they are nothing but insects.

Disgusting

Gross

Worthless

Creatures

And no one cares.

> *Breath.*

> *Confession*

You know when flies land on your bare legs in the summer?

Or your arms?

Or your toes?

And you swat them away so they can buzz off to go bug someone else?

Sometimes, I would just let the fly crawl on me.

The little pitter and soft touch of its legs was comforting on my skin.

No one ever touched me so lightly.

I felt more connected to that fly than anyone else.

Ow!

Something bites her leg and she goes to wipe the blood away, but decides to taste it instead;

it tastes good.

She begins to eat her finger.

Then begins to eat her hand.

She is consuming herself.

She is halfway to standing then –

She is suddenly somewhere else.

Confusion.

I feel like I'm supposed to be doing some –

Become MANIDOONS.

MANIDOONS THREE: BLUE NAILS

MANIDOONS: Shhh – can you hear it?

The sound of skin

Skin on skin

The screeching of fingertips dragging

Of blue nails digging

Digging in

The shuffling of hand over knee

Of knee over hand

The stretch of her desire

It's sinking

Sinking into her now

She's soaking in it

Dancing in it

Drowning

Drowning in it

She's drowning

ESCAPE

Become human.

THE GIRL: You have a car!?

She runs and sits in the passenger seat of her boyfriend's car.

He had a car

He had a car and an apartment and drugs and I was fifteen so I fell in love with him.

And he took me away from the rez. Took me away from all that pain and all the ants and the food.

He took me away and gave me something else

He gave me

Escape

> *She gets high and begins to repeat a high movement/gesture sequence.*
>
> *MANIDOONS comes through her hands.*

The highs filled my lungs, my body

Travelling like a smooth hitchhiker down the highway

Trusting everyone to lead him the right way

And always

Getting

Where

He needed

To go

Everything felt like it was going to be OK

Like it was always going to be OK

I wanted to live in that rainbow with him forever

Years went by and we started …

> *She is choked.*

Then I started …

She is tense and full of self-loathing.

She gets up, ready to leave him.

But can't.

Confession.

Sometimes
I would just sit
Like for hours
On the kitchen floor
Because it was like … it was like safe, you know?
I spent a lot of time on the floor
Sometimes
It's just easier to stay there

She repeats the high movement.

And then the waves would come
And wash over me
With that fuzzy, numb relief

Sometimes
He would sit with me
Sometimes

But it wasn't enough.

It was never enough.

Did you know that when you're abandoned, no amount of love is enough?

I just need –

Movement score.

How many ways does colonization make us hurt ourselves or turn on ourselves?

Prick, prick, prick

just a little prick

a little action

in and out

like tattoos

Or bee stings

Like lying in a field of flowers

Bees covering my arms

Each one stinging me, then dying

Stinging me, then dying

Stinging me, then dying

Surrounding my body

Until there is nothing left

And I'm covered in bee carcasses and stingers

A warm, fuzzy coffin

It's like

It's like

It's like I can't

It's like I can't get enough

It hurts in my blood

It hurts in my brain

In my eyes

My thoughts betray me

And the only way to get it all to stop is … (*Gasp.*)

I used to lie

It was the only way I could keep … (*Gasp.*)

I was so proud

So proud of my scars

When they showed up like white lines of…

> *Something is caught in her throat – she coughs.*
>
> *She pulls it out and throws it out and away.*

Like white lines of coke on my –

> *It crawls quickly back up her body and back into her throat.*
>
> *(It crawls by way of MANIDOONS manifesting itself in her hand.)*
>
> *Her mouth is covered by her own hand, she struggles to remove it.*

On my –

> *Her mouth is covered.*

On my –

Her mouth is covered.

On my –

Her mouth is covered.

On my arms

Rush of endorphins.

Calm.

It was the first real thing I felt like I accomplished on my own

She moves her hands down her body.

LADYBUG

Her baby is born – physical birth gesture.

She cups her hands together holding her "baby" as if it were a tiny ladybug.

Until she came along
My little ladybug.
It made me even fatter but I didn't care.
I didn't even know I was pregnant.
Ever funny, eh?

She circles the witnesses and shows them her new baby.

She was the most beautiful thing I ever saw in my whole life

She was perfect

Perfect

She breathed new life into me

And somehow, *she* became my escape

She became my rainbow

Everything was different

Everything was ... clear

She made me fight everything

Everything inside of me

She made me try harder, you know?

I remember when she laughed for the first time

Like bubbles exploding from her tiny mouth

I watched her sweet face as she fed from my breast

The blood

And rawness

Just made me feel more ...

Well – it just made me *feel*

Bathing her felt like bathing myself

We both became clean

Baptized by a bond

And she loved her baths

I would sing and she would splash and giggle

She begins to bathe her daughter and sing.

Anangoohns anangoohns waasikose
Indoowaanendam awenen giin
Iwidi waasaa giizhigong
Dibishkoo waasikose

She takes her out and holds her.

I wrapped her in blue blankets
Swaddled like she could have been the baby
Jesus
She was mine and I loved her so m –

The baby is taken from her.

She was six months, three days, and five hours
old when they took her.

My neighbour called them and told them that
she thought me and my boyfriend were high
and that she suspected we were high a lot and
that she didn't think it was a safe environment
for a baby to be in.

That crazy white cunt didn't leave her house for
months and let her kids run loose around the
neighbourhood when two of them had scabies
and they take *my* baby away!?

I was fucking sober!

Beat.

Then he left me too

My highway

My man

I'm not any good no more

She repeats the high movement.

And

And then the feeling called me back in

Biting my toes

Nibbling at my skin

Rushing and warming

Seducing me

Whispering

I just need …

I just need …

*Her MANIDOONS hand starts creeping up
her body.*

I thought about my Mother.

And how she let them take me…

She stops the hand.

No.

I can't…

A battle.

She moves as if trying to rub tar off of her body.

A physical sequence – dancing her battle.

So

I answered all their questions

And sometimes I told them lies

I attended all their meetings

Speaking was hard

I drank all their coffee

And smiled in their faces

I avoided all of my friends

Except when I couldn't

I had to go on welfare

And tried to get a job

But no one

Wants

To hire

A Native woman

Clinic after spiral after clinic after spiral after clinic after spiral

I sank and rose

And ebbed and flowed

I danced a battle

I presented myself

Nice nice hair

Nice nice clothes

Nice nice handshake

Nice nice goals

I danced

I danced

I danced

I danced on the line of recovery and the moves were just enough to get her back in my arms again

She holds her daughter in her hands.

My little ladybug.

This time

It's just us

Just us two

Everything is going to be OK

Beat

I'm doing the best I can

She hears her daughter laugh.

My favourite sound in the world

Is her laughing

Like my Auntie's laugh

Rings in my ear

Loud and cackly like only a Native woman could laugh

In rec centres and bingo halls

Baking and dinner tables

Fireside gatherings

Chimes of throat songs echoing through time
and space

I think I remember my Mother's laugh

Far away

I can barely touch it

Like the tip of a memory

Lost

But I know she laughed

I know she laughed

But there's nothing like *her* laugh

I would tickle her and swing her high and eat
her chubby feet

She looks to her baby in her hands.

As long as she's laughing

We're doing fine

We're OK

I can focus

I can … maintain

My little ladybug

We'll be just fi –

She is being yanked back into the addiction.
She gathers herself and tries again.

We'll be just fi –

She continues to be interrupted by it.

We'll be just fi –

We'll be j –

We'll be –

We'll be just fi –

We'll be jus –

We'll be jus –

We'll be –

She is suddenly somewhere else.
Confusion.

I feel like I'm supposed to be doing some –

Become MANIDOONS.

MANIDOONS FOUR: BLUE VEINS

MANIDOONS: Shh – do you hear that?

We're closer

She's closer

We're closing

Closing in on her

The wind on the outside

Is starting to

Starting to

Turn

We're creeping up

Crawling in

Circling and gnawing on the

On the sweet

Sweet flesh left behind

The blue veins

She's letting us

Letting us in

She's letting us in

SWINGING PARTY

Become human.

THE GIRL is in a park at night.

She is not well.

She is searching for something.

She reaches out to the witnesses as other people at the park.

Will they reach back?

Hey

Hey no

Hey c'mon

Hey

Can I just…

Can I just have a little…?

I just need

Hey

Hey

I just need to feel the air

I need it to fill me

Let's go

Go

Go to the place where they swing all night

Off of tree tops

And swirling ceilings

I just need to feel the…

I want the wind, you know?

The wind wind wind

Blow me back

Back to the beginning

Back to the…

(*Gasp.*)

The moon

Look at her

Look

She's got a feather in her hair

(*Laughs then stops.*)

Look out

Look out for the traps

They feed them poison to bring back to the Queen

Did you – did you know?

Hey

Let's go

C'mon c'mon

I'll only take what I can replace

I just need to

I just need to

Feel good again

Fill me

Fill me up

I am a bottomless well!

I just need…

I just need…

I just –

CANDYMAN

A support group.

THE MOTHER sits in a chair.

THE MOTHER: What the fuck was his name?

That guy that useta come around?

(*Remembers.*)

Robert!

Robert Gill.

He was friends with my cousin.

A mechanic in the city.

Good with his hands.

Mmm

He had a thing for Native girls.

My cousin Charmane useta call him candyman

Robert "candyman" Gill.

He always had something for us

Something for us girls.

We'd go down by the tracks – a bunch of us, just partying, eh?

This one time, the cops caught us.

Just they came down and got right in our faces, you know? Just got right up in our business about trespassing and public intoxication and that

Especially us girls – they were these two white guys, they got real rough and ... kinda handsy with us and fuckin Robert just pulls down his pants and pisses on the one guy's shoe.

Oh he was mad, boy.

They both jumped on him and put the cuffs on him and his fuckin dick was still hanging out, eh?

Me and the girls just ran all the way back to the rez just laughing.

His Dad got him out the next day and we were back by the tracks a few hours later.

I never thanked him for pissing on that cop's shoe.

He jumped off a bridge when we were 17

Beat.

He was so high he jumped off a bridge

I forgot about that…

Beat.

Hey, when's lunch?

I know, I know, I just … I'm hungry

No, I'm not upset, I'm just – hungry

Well, can I go make a fucking sandwich or something?

Yeah, I know I … don't fucking touch me!

Don't you fucking lay a hand on me.

Fuck off!

Fuck off!

FUCK OFFFFFFF!!!!!

> *She is grabbed and wrestled to the floor by security.*

WINGS

> *THE GIRL sits on the floor of her kitchen, a single light bulb flickering.*

THE GIRL: Sometimes…

I would just sit

> *Her baby begins to cry.*
>
> *She attempts to get up to go get her but can't do it.*

She sees a bug on the floor, picks it up and lets it crawl on her arm.

She watches it until it flies or crawls away.

Have those fireflies … always been able to not fly?

Did someone take their wings?

Or just their like … ability to fly?

Maybe someone come along and hurt them and they feel like –

Like they can't use their wings no more

Can't get off the ground

Can't connect with – with the wind

But they still glow

They still glow

I wish …

I wish I could glow

And fly

But

Sometimes it's just easier to stay on the ground

Sometimes

It's

Just

Easier

She begins to crawl towards the "bathtub."

Sometimes

It's just easier

> *MANIDOONS slowly begins to take over, her voice and body wavering in and out between creature and human.*

> *A battle.*

Sometimes

It's just

Easier

Sometimes

It's just easier

Some – sometimes

It's

Just

Sometimes

It's just –

> *MANIDOONS wins.*

MANIDOONS FIVE: BLUE DOORS

MANIDOONS: Shh

Do you hear it?

The ticking?

The tocking?

The splashing?

The wailing?

The blood boiling in every pore?

She is thrashing

Thrashing here at the blue doors

And windows where we

Where we live

Where we dance

Where we dwell and die

Shh

We live

We live on the inside now

TIRED

> *THE MOTHER wrestles the men off of her and stands.*

THE MOTHER: They ain't gonna give her back to me!

Can't stay sober long enough.

Never could.

You know, they let me see her once?

Yeah.

My girl.

She got so big.

She was so beautiful … and smart!

God, she was so smart.

I didn't know if she recognized me at first.

But then she ran up and gave me a big hug, just wrapped her little arms around my neck and squeezed.

So tight.

She was strong.

Little, but strong.

I wanted to hold onto her forever.

Beat.

I dropped her once, when she was just a baby.

Yeah.

She was wiggling so much.

Such a squirmy baby.

And – and my arms, they just –

She lets her arms drop.

And I dropped her.

Right on the floor.

She screamed so loud.

Never heard her cry like that before.

It scared the shit outta me, man.

That girl deserves better.

She deserves better than me.

She leaves the circle.

Leaves group.

They won't even fucking help me here

I just want –

I just want help, you know?

I just want help.

I'm tired, man.

The streets are …

I'm just so tired.

> *She walks off into the darkness.*

WALKING

> *THE GIRL is carrying her baby to the bathroom for her bath.*
>
> *She moves with lethargy.*
>
> *She places her baby in the bathtub and begins to do the bathing sequence.*
>
> *She sings.*
>
> *At some point during the song, her MANIDOONS hand begins to creep and pull her away.*
>
> *She tries to fight it momentarily but eventually it wins, both hands infected, crawling up her body.*
>
> *It affects her voice.*

THE GIRL: Anangoohns anangoohns waasikose

Indoowaanendam awenen giin

Iwidi waasaa giizhigong

Dibishkoo waasikose

Anangoohns anangoohns waasikose

Indoowaanendam awenen giin

> *She walks away from the bathtub, leaving the baby behind.*
>
> *She stands in a doorway.*

It's so easy, isn't it?

To just walk.

To put one foot in front of the other and – and just walk.

We know it's walking because it's what we're told.

And we know how to because it's what we were taught.

I feel like I might forget how to walk.

Like, at any minute I'll look down at my feet and *they'll* forget what to do and *I'll* forget what to do and I'll fall.

I will fall.

If someone asks me what happened, I will have to say

"I forget how to walk."

(*Gasp.*)

I feel like I'm supposed to be doing something…

(*Gasp.*)

My little ladybug loves her baths

> *Realization – horror.*

*THE GIRL runs back to the tub where she left
her daughter, who has, indeed, slipped under
the water.*

A physical score.

*Her movements are slow – as if underwater
herself – as she pulls her daughter out, trying
to get her to breathe.*

Blue;

the colour of frost on a foxglove

And the tint on your skin

I scooped you up

Your wet wet body

I just needed you to breathe

I just needed you to cry

To laugh

Your wet wet body

I just needed –

Breath.

You coughed up liquid and what felt like an
insect trying to crawl back into your mouth

Your throat

Blue;

The colour of your lips

Of small lips quivering and cold

I wrapped you like the baby Jesus

Trying to bring your skin back to life

Back to the sun earth colour it is

Trying to warm

And warm

And warm

They breathe together.

She speaks to her daughter.

I held you close to me

For the second time, I gave you life

The both of us covered in screams and tears and water

I saw those beetles in your sweet curls

They're readying you for a battle

The both of us

Two silverfish

Circling the drain

And *you* came back to me

And I...

You know – I only left the bathroom for just a minute...

Beat.

Judgement.

I'm not any good no more

CONSEQUENCES

> *THE GIRL runs to the centre of the circle – to the hospital, looking for someone to help her.*

> *And the baby is taken from her.*
> *Again.*

THE GIRL: And they took her away again and … and …

> *THE GIRL is suspended in light.*
> *Questioned.*

I – I only left the bathroom …
No you – you don't know
You don't know what I …
It was just a –

> *Something is caught in her throat.*
> *She pulls it out and throws it away.*

It was just a –

> *It crawls back in.*
> *She coughs.*
> *Swallows it.*

Give her back
Give her back to me!
She's mine!

Give her back!

> *She swats out and then is grabbed and arrested.*
>
> *Physical arrest sequence.*

No! Let go of me!

You're hurting me!

Let go!

> *She is thrown down.*
>
> *Incarcerated.*

WITHDRAWAL

> *THE GIRL sits.*
>
> *Her skin starts to itch.*
>
> *It gets itchier and itchier.*
>
> *MANIDOONS begins to waver in and out of her voice.*

THE GIRL: I can feel them

I can feel them in my skin

They're crawling on me

All over me

They're swarming my body and eating me from
the inside out

I can feel their teeth ripping into me

It hurts

It hurts

I want

I want my M –

It hurts

You're poisoning me!

You're covering me with roaches while I sleep.

I choke on them in the morning.

I can't breathe!

I can't breathe!

I am being eaten into nothing

I *am* nothing

I am *nothing*

I am –

I am –

Swatted.

Slapped.

Squished.

Flicked.

Poisoned.

Choked.

Swatted.

Slapped.

Squished.

Flicked.

Poisoned.

Choked.

Swatted.

Slapped…

> *There is a battle between her ancestors and MANIDOONS that happens inside of her body.*
>
> *She extends and contracts.*
>
> *She suspends.*
>
> *Lifted and dropped.*
>
> *Beauty and trauma all at once.*
>
> *And then all of her ancestors are present.*
>
> *She lies on the floor.*
>
> *Warmth.*

HOPE CYCLE

> *Breath.*
>
> *THE GIRL begins to build herself back up.*
>
> *She looks to the spot THE MOTHER sits in.*

All I wanted was to love my baby the way I wasn't.

But that's what everyone says, isn't it?

"I will not be like my parents."

And then one day, you wake up and you look at yourself in the hallway mirror or catch yourself sweeping the floor a certain way and you realize –

You are just like them.

> *She climbs into the same spot as THE MOTHER and sits.*

> *A support group.*

Hi.

> *Beat.*

Um … I'm scared

I'm scared that she's going to forget me

That she's going to forget my eyes

My hands

My touch on her skin

I'm afraid that she won't hear my voice

You know?

I just …

I don't want her to end up like me

But I'm going to fight

I'm gonna fight for her

Because I know that when you're abandoned, no amount of love is enough.

She deserves enough

We all do

Ni-minjinawez,* my girl. Ni-minjinawez.

THE GIRL dances.

An apology.

An acceptance.

A move forward.

It brings her home to heal.

HOME

She walks the same path she did in the beginning.

Slowly, as she speaks, ancestors begin to reveal themselves.

There's this ... path in the woods near my Auntie's house on the rez

This is where I used to try and catch them;

The glowies ... the fireflies

There is a point in the middle where you can stand and not see any houses no matter which way you look.

Like I can look over there and know that my cousin's house is there but I can't see it, you know?

It's just trees and birds and rays of sunshine in the day and a little moonlight at night

* I'm sorry.

The Girl discovering her healing; "That's where I used to try and catch them; The glowies… the fireflies." Photograph by Dahlia Katz.

And those ... fireflies

It's quiet
It's peaceful
It's ...
It's home

And I wanna bring her here someday.
My little Ladybug
If I ...

When I ...

I want her to see this
And feel this
And know that not everything is shit.

I need her to know that her ancestors are lush
green leaves that give her life.

> *Beat.*

My Auntie used to tell me stories and I ... I never
really paid attention
But being here –

> *Drumbeat.*

I can hear them
I can feel them
Here
They've been here the whole time

She hears her ancestors.
She basks in their strength and love.

She grabs something from the air.
She holds it up in her fist, circling.

And now
I swear
I'm glowing in the dark too

I
Am
Glowing.

I'm glowing.

She goes to open her hand, but it goes dark
before she does.

Fireflies flicker in the dark.

HOPE

The Girl catching the light, hearing her ancestors; "I am glowing."
Photograph by Gilad Cohen.

On Decolonizing Theatre

"That's the way theatre is. It's always been this way."

This was the response I was given when I questioned theatrical practices; whether I asked it out loud or not. Moving to Tkarón:to from Thunder Bay, I had a basic understanding of how the craft worked through community theatre and high school. However, theatre school and being thrust into the industry gave me an even louder perspective. This is what I learned: burnout, imbalance, mental health deterioration, injury, suffering of relationships, sacrifice... It's just not sustainable.

And sure – it might not be this way for some folks. Many are all right with "the way it's always been." But it doesn't work for everyone. And if it doesn't work for everyone, then how can theatre be intersectional?

My issue with the statement of it always being this way, is that it's not true. It's not the way it's always been. Storytelling in its simplest form has existed for years, in many different ways, and I'm currently researching these forms through Indigenous pathways.

I'm interested in finding out what other ways theatre can exist.

I'm interested in decolonizing theatre; dismantling it as a colonial structure.

I'm interested in keeping artists safe and bringing focus back to the heart of theatre: the stories that we're telling.

And the beautiful thing is that I'm not the only one doing this work. Indigenous artists – women, in particular – have been bringing and continue to bring deep Indigenous teachings back to our ways of storytelling. As well as countless other independent artists of colour, who are also working against the grain.

Now, I don't have all the answers. Decolonizing ourselves is messy business. It takes time and patience and a lot of work and an understanding that we might make missteps. It requires a fundamental shift in thinking; collectively and personally.

There are many things wrong with the way the theatre industry runs – we already know that. But we have to start somewhere. Our stories are medicine and the way they are told shouldn't cause suffering. We shouldn't have to "suffer for our art." Storytelling was never meant to be part of a capitalist structure. And I get it – this is the world we live in. We need to be able to live and this is true. But what are other ways that theatre can work? How do we critique a structure even while participating in it? How can we take care of each other in this system? Because we need to. We need to take care of each other. I believe it is through this care and through this questioning of the systems and decolonial thought process that our stories can truly fly.

Chi miigwetch for witnessing our artistic ceremony and for supporting Indigenous theatre and artists in creating a sustainable future for ourselves and our craft.

Yolanda Bonnell, manidoons collective

A Decolonial Act of Resistance

In February of 2020, as we were about to mount our production of *bug* at Theatre Passe Muraille, manidoons collective came to a decision and requested that the critics of Tkarón:to make space for BIPOC voices in the media. We released the following statement:

In our process and work of decolonizing theatre practices, centering marginalized voices, particularly BIPOC (Black, Indigenous and people of colour) is incredibly important. There is an aspect to cultural work – or in our case, artistic ceremony – which does not align with current colonial reviewing practices. In order to encourage a deeper discussion of the work, we are inviting critiques or thoughts from BIPOC folks only. There is a specific lens that white settlers view cultural work through and at this time, we're just not interested in bolstering that view, but rather the thoughts and views of fellow marginalized voices and in particular Indigenous women.

The decision was based on the fact that there is an overwhelming number of white voices critiquing theatre in Tkarón:to. This has led to an incredible amount of problematic and racist reviews on culturally specific theatre. We wanted to provide an opportunity for media outlets to take a look at who they hire and begin relationships with BIPOC writers – specifically Indigenous women. What folks might not know is that reviewers are given free tickets to theatres to see shows that they are reviewing. These critics were more than welcome to attend the show / ceremony, but they were not being provided a ticket and we asked that they kindly refrain from reviewing the show. We received mixed responses about the request – some outlets wanted to talk about why, some didn't respect our wishes and some actually did the work to reach out and hire Indigenous women to speak about the production in a meaningful and impactful way.

The outlets wanted interviews to discuss our decision and the day before our opening, I was interviewed by Tom Power on CBC Radio's *q*. The segment was tweeted out and within a couple of hours, I was hit with a massive amount of online vitriol. The more retweets, the more comments; the more interviews I did, the more hate I received. It was constant. People sought me out on other platforms to message me and call me a racist, make fatphobic comments, mock my 2-Spirit identity – they said I was doing it for attention, all sorts of misinformed, ignorant, hateful things. Articles were released in other languages, from different parts of Turtle Island and beyond. It was a lot. On the other side, I also received a massive amount of support from my peers and loved ones as well as messages of solidarity from women I didn't know – also coming from all over. The reviews from the Indigenous women hired by the media drove home the importance of why we made this decision.

Many articles came out about our controversial decision, which – maybe I was naïve to think that white folks would be all right to give space to us, but I didn't think it was that controversial. In this time now, when we're speaking up against racial injustices, I can only hope that some of these folks are giving a second thought as to why they felt so much resistance that a simple request to uphold the voices and opinions of Indigenous women was so difficult to honour. In the meantime, I encourage every BIPOC artist to remember how much power you have. They will try to take away our voice – our power – but they cannot. It's inside us and their discomfort with us coming to the table means that it's working. And if not – then we make our own table.

Storytelling Workshops

After graduating from theatre school, I knew that I wanted to do some sort of work with Indigenous youth. It felt important. The suicide rates for youth on remote reservations, specifically, are astronomical. Growing up, on my own reservation, I struggled with mental illness and suicide a lot and, as an adult, I watched and continue to watch as government bodies and this country continues to turn away as these children take their own lives. I kept thinking that if I had had access to a creative outlet as a young person, then maybe I wouldn't have struggled as much. Or maybe – the struggle wouldn't have been as tough. I wanted to take the skills I had learned over the years and from theatre school and bring those to Indigenous youth as we toured *bug*, so I created Oshki Misko Minowe – the Young Red Voices storytelling workshop. It's an opportunity for youth to learn new skills to express their creativity through a variety of ways (writing, art, movement, etc.) as well as create a five-minute piece to our creation story / land acknowledgement. They then are invited to perform the story in front of the audience as a prologue to the performance of *bug*.

We typically engage with a local Indigenous liaison who has an existing relationship with the community to encourage youth to sign up. Most recently, we opened the workshops up to Indigenous women as well. These workshops have been some of the most rewarding work I've ever done and I'm incredibly grateful for every youth and woman and non-binary person I've gotten to work with.

Decoding Manidoons

An instruction manual by Yolanda Bonnell

I initially wrote this manual for our design team so they could grasp a deeper understanding of Manidoons' text – their needs and wants hidden within the poetry. So I give this here, but also understand that whatever you, the reader, feel any of these words mean to you – you are also correct. Nothing only means one thing in this story.

MANIDOONS 1: BLUE PAVEMENT

MANIDOONS: Shhh – can you hear it?

>Crawling
>
>Crawling on the
>
>Blue pavement
>
>Crawling
>
>On the
>
>Floors
>
>On her skin
>
>Making her
>
>Making her move
>
>The sounds of escape
>
>The pitter
>
>Pitter of helplessness

The patter

Patter of despair

The tip and the toe of running towards the thing
she loves the most in this world

Of thirst and

Need and

Want and –

So this is the first time we hear from Manidoons. I think
about the end of the play when she pulls the baby out of the
water and says that she sees those beetles in her sweet curls.
Indicating that the baby will have her own "bug" or version of
Manidoons that she will have to fight. For me, this Manidoons
is viewing The Girl as a young child; a toddler.

The image of the blue pavement originally comes from my
grandparents' basement. The floors were a blue cement and I
used to have reoccurring nightmares about it that stemmed from
my sexual abuse. So I gave her blue pavement floors for her to
watch bugs crawl on as a child.

So the opening lines of "crawling on the blue pavement –
crawling on the floors" is Manidoons talking about themselves
crawling towards her and if an infant saw a bug coming towards
her, they would move away "making her move" and the sounds
of her escape, pitter patter of her feet and tip toeing and running
for her Mother and the thirst and need and want for love and
affection and safety.

MANIDOONS 2: BLUE SKY

MANIDOONS: Shhh

Do you hear that?

It's so loud

Loud and pounding

Those raindrops

Thundering sobs from the

dark blue sky

I made it across the

Across the room

Before it began

But not before I tasted her

Infected her

She doesn't know I'm here, yet

It just takes so long to

Long to

Crawl

To slither

I wish

I wish I had wings instead

Okay, so she's older now and right before this, she's talking about being moved around to different foster homes, and directly after this, she's talking about her addiction to food.

"Loud and pounding those raindrops – thundering sobs from the dark blue sky"

Manidoons is talking about her tears. Her tears and sobs are so loud, it feels as if they are coming from the skies. Her tears are coming from being taken away and moved around and feeling isolated and lonely and filling that void with food. "I made it across the room before it began," so they caught up with her when she wasn't looking, really. The truth is, Manidoons is technically already inside of her because she was born from that cycle, just like her baby. But there are always outside forces that magnify these things and push us towards negative coping mechanisms. Manidoons, the physical presence, is a manifestation of that feeling of the awful things and cycles she's caught in, the closer and stronger they get, the closer and stronger

Manidoons gets.

So at this point, The Girl is in a vulnerable state and that allows Manidoons to get close enough to taste her and infect her with that need for more. And at the same time, Manidoons now has a need for more as they have tasted her.

And the want for wings to just make it easier to always get to her.

MANIDOONS 3: BLUE NAILS

MANIDOONS: Shhh – can you hear it?

> The sound of skin
>
> Skin on skin
>
> The screeching of fingertips dragging
>
> Of blue nails digging
>
> Digging in
>
> The shuffling of hand over knee
>
> Of knee over hand
>
> The stretch of her desire
>
> It's sinking
>
> Sinking into her now
>
> She's soaking in it
>
> Dancing in it
>
> Drowning
>
> Drowning in it
>
> She's drowning

So at this point, The Girl has just spoken about the first time she had sex and the subsequent sexual encounters at a really young age.

"The sound of skin on skin" is the sound of her body against someone else's.

There is an actual double meaning with the fingernails.

"The screeching of fingertips dragging" – so I actually use tips instead of nails – this one runs a bit deep but when someone touches you, or runs their hands on your skin – it actually is their fingertips dragging. A lot of these boys/men she didn't want to be with, so the touch of their fingertips on her skin is "screeching" because it's unpleasant. And for Manidoons – someone else is touching her and they can't touch her all the time, so it's frustrating.

The "blue nails digging in" is the double meaning as, of course, it means nails digging in backs for sex but it also is a coping mechanism of self-harm to dig your nails into your palms. In truth, she is using sex as self-harm, so it works in both of those ways.

"The shuffling of hand over knee/over hand" is actually a contortion of body – how she's feeling on the inside but also what she's doing on the outside – it actually indicates crawling.

She's finding out what she likes and what she thinks she likes so "the stretch of her desire" is actually her bending what her desire could be to making it what she wants – the feeling of *being* desired. And that's the feeling she dances in and drowns in. The feeling of being wanted for her body gives her something to latch on to. At least someone wants her for something so she takes that feeling and drowns in it and Manidoons sees that weakness and knows that they can use that.

MANIDOONS 4: BLUE VEINS

MANIDOONS: Shh – do you hear that?

> We're closer
>
> She's closer
>
> We're closing
>
> Closing in on her
>
> The wind on the outside
>
> Is starting to

Starting to

Turn

We're creeping up

Crawling in

Circling and gnawing on the

On the sweet

Sweet flesh left behind

The blue veins

She's letting us

Letting us in

She's letting us in

So we're at the point in the story now where Manidoons has nearly completely infected her. Right before this, the baby was taken, she got her back but began using again – "we would be just fine" – so she's spiralled back.

Manidoons has begun using "we" as her addiction grows, there's more of a larger presence and the need to express that it's overwhelming – an infestation. Manidoons recognizes that they are getting closer as she's actually getting closer to them as well. It's as if she's coming towards them.

"The wind on the outside is starting to turn," so Manidoons can see the change in her behaviour. Having her child taken from her was the first indicator that she might be turning out like her Mother DESPITE the fact that it actually wasn't her fault. She can't shut down that internal monologue. Those fears cause the spiral that changes her completely back to using, which is what Manidoons sees. And that allows them to "creep up and crawl in and circle and gnaw on her," so they're starting to eat through her skin to get inside. "The sweet flesh left behind – the blue veins" is the health and vitality that she's leaving behind. She's opening herself up to the infection at this point.

MANIDOONS 5: BLUE DOORS

MANIDOONS: Shh

Do you hear it?

The ticking?

The tocking?

The splashing?

The wailing?

The blood boiling in every pore?

She is thrashing

Thrashing here at the blue doors

And windows where we

Where we live

Where we dance

Where we dwell and die

Shh

We live

We live on the inside now

So this one is the last one and is at our climax. Manidoons is basically setting the scene for what is about to happen. They can see where this whole thing is heading: from the scene prior where the baby is crying and she starts crawling to go get her and then Manidoons shows up. They can see that she's going to give the baby a bath to stop her from crying and that she will feel the need to get high and that she will leave. They have recognized her patterns and know her so well at this point.

So –

The ticking and tocking is the minutes that are passing as the baby is in the tub.

The splashing and wailing are her crying in the tub.

The blood boiling in every pore is the panic from both of

them when she pulls her out.

The thrashing and the doors and windows of where they live, dance, dwell, and die is basically Manidoons seeing her come to them now. There is an exchange and a past the point of no return. She leaves the tub to "thrash at the doors" of where they live to get high.They've opened the door and now they live inside of her.

As a final note, as dark as it gets here at the end – it's important to note that The Girl finds her hope and function despite having a Manidoons living inside of her.